EVANGELIZE *with* ME

EVANGELIZE WITH ME
Copyright © 2023 by Ariston Pallugna Awitan Jr., M.D.

Published in the United States of America
ISBN   Paperback: 979-8-89091-201-5
ISBN   eBook: 979-8-89091-202-2

All rights reserved. No part of this publication may be reproduced, stored in a retrieval system or transmitted in any way by any means, electronic, mechanical, photocopy, recording or otherwise without the prior permission of the author except as provided by USA copyright law.

The opinions expressed by the author are not necessarily those of ReadersMagnet, LLC.

ReadersMagnet, LLC
10620 Treena Street, Suite 230 | San Diego, California, 92131 USA
1.619. 354. 2643 | www.readersmagnet.com

Book design copyright © 2023 by ReadersMagnet, LLC. All rights reserved.

Cover design by Ericka Obando
Interior design by Daniel Lopez

EVANGELIZE
with ME

ARISTON PALLUGNA AWITAN JR., M.D.

ReadersMagnet, LLC

Contents

INTRODUCTION VII
TWO WORDS THAT DEFINE CHRISTIANITY XIII
WHAT REALLY MATTERS...XVII
ABOUT THIS BOOK XXI
DEDICATION XXIII
CHAPTER ONE 1
CHAPTER TWO 3
CHAPTER THREE 8
CHAPTER FOUR 13
CHAPTER FIVE.. 16
CHAPTER SIX... 22
CHAPTER SEVEN 29
MY OWN SELF-TALK DAILY 53
ACKNOWLEDGMENT 67
ABOUT THE AUTHOR 59
REFERENCES 63

Introduction

My Favorite Scripture Verses from the New International Version and the Revised Standard Version

John 3:16

16 For God so loved the world that he gave his one and only Son, that whoever believes in him shall not perish but have eternal life.

Mark 12:28-31

The Greatest Commandment

28 One of the teachers of the law came and heard them debating. Noticing that Jesus had given them a good answer, he asked him, "Of all the commandments, which is the most important?"

29 "The most important one," answered Jesus, "is this: 'Hear, O Israel: The Lord our God, the Lord is one."

30 'Love the Lord your God with all your heart, with all your soul, with all your mind and with all your strength.'

31 The second is this: 'Love your neighbor as yourself.' There is no commandment greater than these."

Matthew 28:16-20

The Great Commission

16 Then the eleven disciples went to Galilee, to the mountain where Jesus had told them to go.

17 When they saw him, they worshiped him; but some doubted.

18 Then Jesus came to them and said, "All authority in heaven and on earth has been given to me.

19 Therefore go and make disciples of all nations, baptizing them in the name of the Father and of the Son and of the Holy Spirit,

20 and teach them to obey everything I have commanded you. And surely, I am with you always, to the very end of the age."

Psalm 23:1-6

1 "The Lord is my shepherd, I shall not want;

2 He makes me lie down in green pastures;
He leads me beside still waters;

3 He restores my soul.
He leads me in paths of righteousness;
for His name's sake.

4 Even though I walk through the valley of the shadow of death,
I fear no evil;
for thou art with me;
thy rod and thy staff,
they comfort me.

5 Thou preparest a table before me in the presence of my enemies; thou anointest my head with oil, my cup overflows.

6 Surely goodness and mercy shall follow me all the days of my life; and I shall dwell in the house of the Lord forever."

Matthew 6:19-21

Treasures in Heaven

19 "Do not store up for yourselves treasures on earth, where moths and vermin destroy, and where thieves break in and steal.

20 But store up for yourselves treasures in heaven, where moths and vermin do not destroy, and where thieves do not break in and steal.

21 For where your treasure is, there your heart will be also."

Two Words That Define Christianity

"I would pick the words GIVE and SERVE." That's what Jesus did. "I did not come to be served but to serve and to give my life as a ransom for many." (Matthew 20:28) The words **give** and **serve** summarizes the Christian life. In James 1:22 we read, "Be doers of the word and not hearers only."

Furthermore, the Bible tells us that the number one priority of life is that we should give our lives in serving God and others."

One of the most important reasons is **we will be rewarded for eternity.**

Maybe you have read this verse before in John 12:26 which says, "My Father will honor anyone who serves me." This is a reward for those who are willing to give themselves in serving God and others. They will receive the crown of life which God has promised to those who love and serve Him. Jesus would tell us one day when we come to Him, *"Well done, good and faithful servant, enter into the joy of my Father which has been prepared for you before the foundation of the world. Come on in."*

(Quoted from Living the Christian Life from a Chaotic World by Rev. Reggie M. Dancel Jr.)

What Really Matters

"As I live the rest of my golden years, I now realize that it is not really our APTITUDE (I.Q. Intelligent Quotient) but our ATTITUDE, that determines our ALTITUDE. The greatest achievement one can have in this life is to have Jesus Christ as Lord and Savior of one's life.
(Quoted from Autobiography of Rev. Reggie M. Dancel Jr.)

Malachi 3:10-12

10 "Bring the whole tithe into the storehouse, that there may be food in my house. Test me in this," says the Lord Almighty, "and see if I will not throw open the floodgates of heaven and pour out so

much blessing that there will not be room enough to store it.

11 I will prevent pests from devouring your crops, and the vines in your fields will not drop their fruit before it is ripe," says the Lord Almighty.

12 "Then all the nations will call you blessed, for yours will be a delightful land," says the Lord Almighty."

So we know what God wants us to do. We can be creative in our own way to share the Gospel. For myself I chose to write this book, "EVANGELIZE WITH ME". I am promoting my favorite charities to encourage people to donate and support them. Hopefully in their own creative ways, they can also share the good news to their own friends and also encourage them to do the same down the line. I encourage each of them to share with at least three of their friends. Hopefully by reading this book they will be encouraged to donate and support any or all of these charities with tax-deductible donations.

May God Bless us with our efforts.
Ariston Pallugna Awitan, Jr., M.D.

About This Book

This book, "EVANGELIZE WITH ME" is a compilation of my favorite charities and some important chapters of my favorite books for the purpose of sharing the Gospel to the world. This is one way that I chose to share the good news to people who are interested in reading books recommended by their friends. It is my hope with a strong faith that they would share the contents and encourage them to donate and support these different charities which effectively promote and share the Gospel. This is the activity I chose to spend the rest of my life on planet Earth. I would highly appreciate it if you join me within the mission.

Dedication

This book is dedicated to the following:

To my children; Ariston III, Cecilia, Edward and Brian;

To my grandchildren; Ariston IV, Matthew, Jade Ivy, Nicholas, Ava-Josephine, and Marlena;

To my great grandsons; Nico, Joseph, Marcelo and Robert;

Also, I dedicate this book to my first wife, Dr. Josefina Capistrano Awitan; to my second wife, Donna Wray Frolich; to my third wife. Juliet Gran Ringer; to my fourth wife, Josephine Wheeler Phillips;

to Ray Wheeler, the only son of Josephine Wheeler Phillips; To my daughter-in-law, Joanne Foote, the wife of my son, Ariston III; Leah Wells, the ex-wife of my son Brian; Wendy Martin, ex-wife of my son Edward and mother of my grandson Nicholas; Iris, the mother of my 3 great-grandsons; and Trizia Vargas, ex-wife of my grandson, Nicholas.

All of the above have given me the satisfaction for having worked hard, realized my dreams and achieved my full potential.

With all my love,

APA, Jr. M.D.

Chapter One

ETERNAL WORD TELEVISION NETWORK

HISTORY

EWTN Global Catholic Network, in its 40th year, is the largest religious media network in the world. EWTN's 11 global TV channels are broadcast in multiple languages 24 hours a day, seven days a week to over 350 million television households in more than 145 countries and territories. EWTN platforms also include radio services transmitted through SIRIUS/XM, iHeart Radio, and over 500 domestic and international AM & FM radio affiliates;

a worldwide shortwave radio service; one of the largest Catholic websites in the U.S.; electronic and print news services, including Catholic News Agency, "The National Catholic Register" newspaper, and several global news wire services; as well as EWTN Publishing, its book publishing division.

When Eternal Word Television Network (EWTN) was launched on Aug. 15, 1981, many felt there would be little demand for a Catholic network. In fact, when Mother M. Angelica, a cloistered nun, fulfilled a promise to our Lord in the early 1960s by founding Our Lady of Angels Monastery in Irondale, Ala., she had no idea she would one day found the largest religious media network in the world. Eternal Word Television Network is dedicated to the advancement of truth as defined by the magisterium of the Roman Catholic Church. Your donation is tax-deductible.

Chapter Two

DAUGHTERS OF SAINT PAUL

HISTORY

Pauline is an apostolic ministry of the Daughters of St. Paul. We are consecrated women communicating Christ with our lives. We are 100 years of collaboration among religious, clergy, and laity to help people connect with Jesus Christ and the Church in a secular digital culture.

Paul on the Move

As Daughters of St. Paul, we are missionary sisters sent forth in the spirit of Saint Paul to serve the Church and bring Christ to the world through the most effective means of communication. Globally, there are over 1,900 Media Nuns serving in over 50 countries. The Daughters of St. Paul will continue to collaborate with and support these.

FAQs

As missionary sisters sent forth in the spirit of Saint Paul, we are always on the move to proclaim the Gospel. After taking stock of the many opportunities we have to evangelize with the communications media today, as well as the reality of the gifts and talents of our sisters and the young women entering our community, we are reconfiguring our presence across the U.S. and Canada.

About

The Pauline Center for Media Studies (PCMS) is a project of the Daughters of St. Paul. Its focus is to develop and encourage media literacy/media mindfulness within the context of culture, education, and faith formation. The PCMS, founded by Sister Rose Pacatte, FSP, began in Boston in 1995 and moved to Los Angeles in 2006.

Choir

For almost thirty years, the sisters of the Daughters of St Paul Choir have shared the consoling message of God's love through choral recordings. It's a ministry of prayer for us: As we sing, we pray for all those whom our voices will reach through different channels, whether on the radio or on a movie soundtrack, in a car or on the phone on Spotify or through a CD in a hospital room. And what a consolation it is for us when people tell us of the hope they have found (or of lives saved from suicide) through our music!

Film Reviews

Ask the Sisters to pray for you. OUR MISSION, The Daughters of Saint Paul are an international congregation of women religious called, consecrated, and sent to evangelize in the spirit of St. Paul through our lives and all forms of media. We are present in 50 nations with over 2,500 Sisters carrying out the Pauline mission around the world.

Who We Are - Daughters of St. Paul on the Move

Like Paul, we are overwhelmed by the love of Jesus, "who died for me". We feel impelled to tell about the Lord, who has "shown us great mercy". Daily, we seek to "put on the Lord Jesus Christ," to be gradually transformed in him. We begin each day at mass, which roots us in the gift of love, the Eucharist. A place where young women in the USA and Canada who are discerning Pauline religious life can connect Daughters of St. Paul.

The Mission of the Daughters of St. Paul

The Daughters of St. Paul carry out a new form of evangelization by living and witnessing to the Faith through communications. As Daughters of Saint Paul, we journey alongside humanity, seeking to respond to each person's yearnings with the loving invitation of Christ. Today, we witness how the world is in anguish, desperate for God.

Chapter Three

JOY AND CAREGIVING FOUNDATION ST. ANTHONY DEVELOPMENT AND LEARNING CENTER OF BULACAN

HISTORY

Our mission is to make impactful giving easier for all.

Since 2001, we've empowered millions of donors by providing free access to data, tools, and resources to guide philanthropic decision-making.

With nearly 200,000 charities rated, our comprehensive ratings shine a light on the cost-effectiveness and overall health of a charity's programs, including measures of stability, efficiency, and sustainability. The metrics inform donors of not just where their dollars are going but what their dollars are doing.

Like the organizations we rate, we're a 501(c)(3) nonprofit, too. We don't charge the charities we evaluate, ensuring our ratings remain objective. In turn, we depend on the generosity of individuals, foundations, and corporations to fund our programs.

Our Methodology

Find out how we rate charities, issue Advisories, and curate lists of organizations working across various causes and issues to help you find and support trustworthy, effective charities that align with your passions and values.

Our Team

Making impactful giving easier for all is a collaborative effort that relies on the hard work and dedication of individuals inside and outside of Charity Navigator.

Thought Leadership & News

Beyond ratings, we want to ensure that you have access to essential information about the nonprofit sector and our work.

Financials and Policies

Learn how we steward your contribution to advance the ratings and resources millions of donors use to inform their giving.

Careers

Discover opportunities to work at Charity Navigator and apply today.

Press Room

Explore our recent press coverage.

Our Values

These are the beliefs and principles that guide Charity Navigator and our team.

Leadership

We dream big and strive toward making the seemingly impossible possible, lifting the sector as we go.

Collaboration

We collaborate internally and externally to accelerate our work and achieve more together.

Equity

We stand for equity, diversity, and inclusion within our organization and through our evaluations and guidance.

Fairness

We assume good intent, leading with trust within our organization and through our work to catalyze giving wherever there is need.

Usefulness

We provide fair, transparent evaluations, and valuable tools to enable a diverse set of donors to find and support an ever-greater number of nonprofits they can trust.

Chapter Four

ASSOCIATION OF MARIAN HELPERS

HISTORY

Greetings from Eden Hill - the grounds of the Marian Helpers Center and the National Shrine of the Divine Mercy. This location in Stockbridge, Massachusetts, is the spiritual home of the Association of Marian Helpers.

Officially established in 1944, the Association began as a small group of friends who believed in and supported the work of the Marian priests and brothers. Now with some 1.5 million strong members, the Association is a spiritual benefit society that continues to prayerfully and financially support the Congregation of Marian Fathers of the Immaculate Conception.

Enrolled members share in the spiritual benefits of the Holy Masses, prayers, and good works of the Marians. Through this website, our Marian Helper member magazine, and various other materials, members receive information about the Marian family and are encouraged to strive for personal holiness. You can enroll yourself or others, living and deceased.

Remembering the souls of the departed is an important ministry of my Congregation. Many people have come to know us from our remembrance cards and enrollment folders.

But we also have many other ministries and services:

- A toll-free intercessory prayer line.
- Novenas throughout the year.
- Votive candles lit for prayer intentions.
- Mail order catalogue and online catalog.
- Pilgrimages guided by a Marian.

- Print materials to promote devotion to Mary and Divine Mercy.

(Quoted from the Website of Association of Marian Helpers.)

Chapter Five

PRIESTS OF THE SACRED HEART AND SACRED HEART MONASTERY

HISTORY

The Sacred Heart Monastery with its iconic round chapel, Sacred Heart Monastery is considered a showpiece of the mid-century architectural movement. The structure was designed by architect Henry R. Slaby and completed in 1968.

The monastery houses the Sacred Heart Seminary and School of Theology, North America's largest seminary specializing in the preparation of men over 30 for the priesthood. Catholic dioceses and religious orders throughout the U.S. and Canada choose Sacred Heart for the education of their future priests. The seminary also provides an English-as-a-Second-Language program for students from overseas and offers a Master of Arts program to prepare men and women for lay ecclesial ministry. Since 1932 we've remained dedicated to the formation of effective Church leaders with pastoral hearts.

The life of Sacred Heart Retreat, commonly known as "the monastery," has changed along with the lives of the men who have lived here and Holy Cross Province of which it is a part. But, the story of the monastery reflects the history of Holy Cross Province.

Devotion in Action

Our priests and brothers bring God's love into action through ongoing works of mercy – all sustained by your prayers and continuing generosity.

We work among the urban and rural poor in the USA and throughout the world. We care for young immigrant families, aging seniors and many others through parish ministry, food programs, clothing distribution centers and more. Learn about our missionary work.

Mission Galleries

See what your support makes possible.

SCJ News

The Priests of the Sacred Heart (SCJs) are dedicated to spreading devotion to the Sacred Heart of Jesus and rebuilding our world into God's kingdom of justice and love. Our mission is to make known the profound love that Jesus has for all people through prayer, service, education, social action and outreach among the poor and neglected.

How You Can Help

When we accept the abundant love of Jesus and respond to His Sacred Heart with open hearts of our own, we are called to ask: "What more can I do?" There are many ways, through prayer, gifts and action, you can help us share the love of the Sacred Heart.

What Your Gifts Do

Here's how your support enables our mission and ministries. 89% of all support goes directly to program services.

Prayers for Our Military

Find words of comfort and spiritual inspiration to honor those serving our country and for our fallen heroes.

Who We Are

History of the Priests of the Sacred Heart

On 1878, the Priests of the Sacred Heart was founded by Fr. Leo John Dehon in St. Quentin, France. On 1888, the first SCJ foreign mission was established in Ecuador, followed by missions in Brazil and Congo within the next decade. On the year of 1923, the Ministry in the USA begins in a mission among Native Americans in Lower Brule, South Dakota. Six years after, on 1929 Monastery for first American SCJ seminarians opens in Hales Corners, Wisconsin. On 1933, the US Province of the Priests of the Sacred Heart established with headquarters in

Wisconsin. In 1964, 29 members of the SCJ congregation, including a bishop, murdered in a bloody rebellion in Congo. On the year of 1968 the Current Sacred Heart Monastery building dedicated on site across from original structure. On 2013, SCJs inaugurate District of Vietnam, bringing global presence to 41 countries on five continents.

Mission

We are "prophets of love and servants of reconciliation," offering ourselves with Christ to a world which hungers for justice and peace.

Chapter Six

MISSIONARY OF THE POOR

HISTORY

If you've never heard the Lord's Prayer set to Caribbean rhythm, with all the colorful vibrancy and distinctness of reggae percussion and vocals, then you've never heard the ministry of Fr. Richard Ho Lung.

Founder of Missionaries of the Poor (MOP), a pontifical order that began in Kingston, Jamaica, in 1981, the now 81-year-old priest seamlessly melds the weight and tradition of Catholic service with the relaxed vibe and coolness of the Jamaican culture into which he was born and bred.

After 40 years of feeding the world's most destitute while performing in plays and recording Catholic reggae albums to invite people to Christ, all the while raising financial support for the missions, Ho Lung says he has put his trust and confidence in the Lord for His continued guidance and provision. With many people suffering across the world in a year of unprecedented challenges, he continues to stand in the faith, hope and positivity that has carried him through decades of ministry leadership across the globe.

"I want people to raise their hearts to God even in this time of difficulty," said Ho Lung via Zoom in his signature Jamaican accent. "They must be a people of hope. We've got to be more and more focused on the life of Christ and the great, great promises that have been given to all of us."

Since its inception, MOP has supported the elderly, mentally challenged, disabled, HIV-infected and now coronavirus patients. The ministry, maintained through donations and the work of volunteers and benefactors, has expanded to 10 impoverished nations, including Haiti, Indonesia, Uganda, India, the Philippines and Kenya.

With MOP offices located in Canada, the United States and United Kingdom, a large portion of the ministry's funding over the years has come from the generous support of North Americans.

Canada was the first nation outside Jamaica to welcome concerts and plays to raise funds, said Ho Lung.

"The evangelization and the cultural exchange have been tremendous. We've received every possible type of help you can imagine from Canadians. We've gotten funding, food, educational supplies, clothing and volunteers have come to us."

Like many charities, Ho Lung says MOP has seen a significant dip in funding this year due to uncertainties surrounding the coronavirus.

An outbreak at the homes in Kingston has intensified the situation there for the roughly 500 individuals in need. Thankfully, he says of the 75 clients who tested positive for COVID-19, all have recovered or are asymptotic and doing well. Of the brothers staffing the ministry, 22 have also tested positive with one remaining in serious condition.

Currently in the Philippines, what was supposed to be a short visit to the mission there early this year has turned into several months for Ho Lung who has not been able to return to Jamaica due to COVID-19 border closures. He has been staying closely connected with updates from the MOP team currently working on the ground in Jamaica. Though he longs to be back home, he's confident that the faith and resilient spirit that has carried MOP all these years as an organization and as a people will help it through this crisis.

"I was telling the brothers here that in Jamaica when we cry, we end up singing a song as we cry and that spirit never, ever leaves us," said Ho

Lung, who has brought the songs of Jamaica to the missions in the Philippines as well. "I've heard of a number of very good friends who have suffered (from COVID-19), some in cases of death, too. They are people of faith so there's a sense that somehow God is going to carry us to a much, much better place, and we're going to be shocked and surprised at how wonderful it is."

Despite the challenges, Ho Lung has made the best of his time in the Philippines, training the young brothers in the ministry and writing 30 new songs and a new theatrical production. The team hopes that as the situation improves globally and restrictions are lifted, they would be able to bring the production around the world, including to the Greater Toronto Area with its large Jamaican diaspora who have supported MOP productions in the past.

"We have a lot of Jamaicans in our city and a lot of them are very aware of Fr. Ho Lung because I think he would be considered to many a national hero," said Sera Rossi, president of

MOP Canada and a former educator with the Toronto Catholic District School Board. "When he comes up here and he does a show, many people (in the Jamaican community) find out and come to watch. It's absolutely beautiful to see. It's all about helping (MOP) to do the work of helping the poor."

Due to demands of the ministry and the various physical and cognitive conditions suffered by the population living at the Jamaican missions, it has been difficult to get residents to adhere to certain health protocols such as wearing masks, hand washing and social distancing. Despite challenges Ho Lung says he is grateful not to have lost any lives to date and is confident they will have the faith and the strength of character to get to the other side of this.

"Jamaican people are a different kind of people," said Ho Lung. "They, they just keep on going."

As MOP prepares to celebrate 40 years of ministry in 2021, Ho Lung says seeing God's hand through the missions' service to those in need has been and will continue to be the delight of his heart.

"What I glory in the Lord in is the amazing work that He has allowed us to do," said Ho Lung. "We have hundreds and hundreds of people that we care for. To see daily these people rising and having a breakfast prayer and just being joyful and peaceful having water and people to help to take care of them, that gives me absolutely the greatest joy. And then there are the brothers who give their lives over to the service of the poorest of people and that's beautiful.

"Also, I can't deny that the music has been a source of wonder."

In addition to funding, Ho Lung says the greatest need for the mission in Jamaica and around the world is volunteers as many have been unable to serve due to concerns around transmitting the virus to vulnerable family members.

Chapter Seven

I HAVE KEPT THE FAITH - HOME AT LAST

"I have fought a good fight; I have finished the race; I have kept the faith."

The death of a loved one is the most difficult and emotionally draining experience that a family or individual would go through. It is not only emotionally draining and exhausting; it is also financially expensive. It is expensive to die especially here in America. That is the downside.

But the upside is that it is also a good time for relatives and friends who have not seen each other for some time to be together in order to show their love and respect for the one who passed away and to bid their goodbyes for the last time, and at the same time show sympathy or empathy to the bereaved family. So, for our meditation and reflection, I would like to invite your attention to the words of the Apostle Paul found in 2 Timothy 4:6-8 which says, "For I am already being poured out as a drink offering, and the time of my departure is at hand. Vs 7 I have fought a good fight, I have finished the race, I have kept the faith. Vs 8 Finally, there is laid up for me the crown of righteousness, which the Lord, the righteous judge, will give me on that day, and not to me only, but also to all who loved his appearing."

Those words were just like the farewell speech of St. Paul, and in those few words give us the essence of his whole life. He sees himself just like a drink offering, about to be poured out. He used a technical term to use of a cup of wine in Roman sacrifice poured out to the gods.

Though he was going to be executed, he chose to regard this as an offering to God. The Apostle Paul believed that the whole of life is to be regarded as a living sacrifice, holy and acceptable to God. But the problem is that we are not holy and acceptable to God as mentioned in the book of Romans 12:1. That our best sacrificial offering to God is our life itself. The offering must be holy and acceptable to God.

But the problem is that we are not holy and acceptable to God because we are sinners. The Bible tells us that "All have sinned and come short of the glory of God." (Romans 3:23) The good news is we can be made holy and acceptable to God when we repent from our sins and receive God's acceptance and forgiveness.

God became flesh in the person of Jesus Christ to redeem us from our sins and wickedness.

Others would say, "I don't deserve to be forgiven. I have done so many shameful deeds and I am ashamed of myself." The good news is nobody is beyond God's forgiveness. In Isaiah 1:18 we read, "Though your sins be as scarlet, they shall be as white as snow; though they be red like crimson, they shall become like wool." And in the Gospel of John 1:12 it reminds us, "For all who receive him, who believe in his name, he gave them power to become the children of God."

The Bible clearly tells us that anyone who believes in Jesus Christ can become a "living sacrifice, holy and acceptable to God." Our life is that of a living sacrifice.

Then the Apostle Paul states in Verse 6,"The time of my departure is at hand." In essence St. Paul is saying, I am about to die. My time has come. My time to leave this world has come."

Do you know when you are dying? One of the sobering realities of life is that there will come a time when we are going to depart from this life. To put it bluntly - one day you and I are going to die. It's just a matter of time. It's 100 percent sure. It is 100 percent fatal. Some people think that they have all the time to be here, so they might as well enjoy life and do as they please. But life is short. We are here today and gone tomorrow. We may be here for 30, 50, 60, 80 or even 100 years or longer. But that is really short in the eyes of the Lord. That is just like a blink of an eye.

In the First Letter of Peter, it tells us that a thousand years is but a day to the Lord. My wife and I attended the funeral of a 95-year old senior. Some say that it's a long life. But the truth is that life is short. People who are on the receiving end, especially those who are poor and have nothing in life, that dictators, kings and presidents and prime minister and all kinds of rulers are going to live forever. But Emperors die. Kings and presidents die. Dictators die. All of us die. That's why we call death as an equalizer.

Death makes us even whether you are rich or poor. That's the grim reality - we all die. There was a 9-year old girl who wrote God a letter with these words, "Dear God, instead of letting people die and having to make up new ones, why don't you just keep the once you have now? Why does not God arrange it, so we can all live forever now?" That's very interesting thought, isn't it? Suppose we could live forever here on

Earth; what age would you choose? What body would you choose? Would you like to be young forever? That's what the cosmetic industry wants us to be - to remain young, handsome and beautiful the rest of our life so we can keep on buying their products. That's what the plastic surgeons want us to be - to look young forever.

Would you really like to be young forever and never grow old? That baby looking face now would grow old and one day it would wrinkle like prunes. The collagen in our skin is thinning as we get older and it would make our skin wrinkled up. But the question is would you really like to live forever here on earth? Do we have a 90-year old person in our midst? Look at the skin and you know what I mean. Whether we like it or not, one day we are going to depart from this life. We don't really like talking about death in our conversation. Why is that? Because it is not pleasant topic.

We avoid talking about it if we have our own way. But God did not plan that we live here permanently in this life. We are only temporary residents here. To use a traditional term, we are only PILGRIMS here - meaning we are on the go. So while we are here temporarily, how should we live our life? In the writing of the Apostle Paul to the Ephesians 5:15-20 Paul says, "Look carefully on how you live your life, not as unwise man but as wise, making most of the time because the days are evil. Do not be foolish but understand what is the will of the Lord." "Do not be unwise but wise." So who is a wise person? Is it someone who graduated from a university and have earned a bachelor's degree, master's degree or doctoral degree? One can have all those degrees and still not be wise. Just look at those committing crimes and they are some of the most educated people in the country - they are not wise.

Who then is a wise person? A wise person is one who looks at life from God's perspective, one who looks at life from God's point of view. When we look at life from God's perspective, WE REALIZE THAT OUR LIFE IS A GIFT FROM GOD. Others say, "I own my own life, nobody is going to tell me what to do with my life. I do as I please." They are wrong because the Bible tells us as in First Corinthians 6:19-20, "Do you know that your body is the temple of the Holy Spirit, who is in you, whom you have received from God? You are not your own; you were bought at a price.

Therefore, honor God with your body."

Not only our life is a gift from God, but we also realize HOW SHORT LIFE IS. We are here today and gone tomorrow. So we must choose wisdom.

On October 1, 2017 about thirty thousand attended a free country music concert held outside in Las Vegas and Stephen Paddock, a retired accountant and a multimillionaire, a chronic gambler, massacred 59 people and injured more than 500 concert goers. Those who died did not plan to die in Las Vegas. They went there to enjoy and have fun. Instead many lost their lives. Life is short and we don't know when our time comes. That's why Apostle Paul says: "Look carefully at how you live your life not as unwise person but as wise; making the most of the time because the days are evil." The Apostle Paul is simply saying, be prepared. Be on the lookout. You don't have much time. Those were also the words of Jesus when he said, "Be prepared for you don't know when the hour comes. For it will come like a thief at night. Therefore, be watchful, be ready."

A 30-year-old son was visiting his father who was dying of cancer. Cancer is a terrible, terrible disease. It is very destructive. And the father told his son, "My son, don't cry for me. I am about to leave on the most exciting trip of my whole life." Our departure from this life which we call death is actually a trip of all trips, beyond all trips. Because death is a trip to eternity to be with the Lord forever.

Death is a doorway to eternity - to heaven.

To people who don't believe in the Lord, death to them is a grim reality and people are crying and wailing, and their hearts are heavy with grief and full of sadness. But those who have surrendered their life to Jesus Christ,

DEATH IS A TIME FOR CELEBRATION. It is a trip to eternity, to be with the Lord. Death to the believer in Christ is just like going home to heaven. In Philippians 3:20 it says, "For our home is in heaven and there we await the savior Jesus Christ who will transform our lowly body just like his glorious body." We are heaven bound, not earthbound.

Why do we cry when a loved one dies? The main reason we cry, and it is normal to cry when a loved one dies, is because we are going to miss them. They are not coming back. The goodbye is final and permanent. That's why we cry. But we also know they are going to a better place called heaven. This is the reason the departure of a loved one is time for celebration. The loved one is having a trip of all trips, a trip to eternity, to be with the Lord forever.

This is our goal - to be with the Lord forever when our time comes. And it begins here now in this life. The moment we receive Jesus Christ as Lord and savior, we begin to experience his salvation. Not only that but we also experience his closeness and presence each day. Jesus said, "I am with you always even unto the end of age."

It is God's plan that we will be with him in eternity. In John 14:1-6 Jesus said, "Believe in God, believe also in me. In my Father's house are many mansions. If it were not so, would I have told you that I go and prepare a place for you, I will come again and take you their myself. So that where I am, there you may be also."

God's plan is for us to be with the Lord in eternity. Thomas asked, "Lord we don't know the way." Jesus answered, "I am the way, the truth, and the life. No one comes to the Father except through Me."(vs6)

When Susanah Wesley, mother of John Charles Wesley, was dying, she told her children, "When I die, don't cry for me. Sing hymns of praises and thanksgiving to the Lord."

The Apostle Paul gives us some advice as to how we should live our life in verse 7 when he said, *"I have fought a good fight. I have finished the race. I have kept the faith."*

I HAVE FOUGHT A GOOD FIGHT

Paul is telling us that all of us are involved in a game like a contest. That we are like athletes and we are in a race. And in this race, we must do all the best we can. The race is not going to be easy. It is hard and tough. But we must do our best and not give up. We are in a fight, we are in a battle, if you will.

The word FOUGHT in the Greek language literally means "to engage in conflict". But there is a deeper meaning "of fighting a good fight". Our battle or conflict is not with flesh and blood but against principalities, against rulers of darkness of this age, against spiritual hosts of wickedness in the heavenly places as mentioned in Ephesians 6:12.

And the fight and conflict we face is a never ending conflict or struggle against evil. It is a spiritual battle against Satan himself. That is why Paul says, "We must take the whole armor of God and his righteousness so that we may be able to withstand against the wiles of the devil. (Ephesians 6:13) ON OUR OWN WE CANNOT DO IT. WE NEED CHRIST!

St. Paul went through a lot of trials and tribulations. In spite of all that, he could say, "I have fought a good fight," and the astonishing thing is that he could proclaim his victory in Christ by saying, "Yet in all these things, we are more than conquerors through Christ who loved us." (Romans 8:37)

Some of us are facing a good fight right now in their life.

They are engaged in a battle right now, if you have high blood pressure problem, diabetes, heart problem, cancer, etc., etc., life is beginning to close in and you are in a battle for your life. Like the Apostle Paul, we can say with him, I HAVE FOUGHT A GOOD FIGHT.

But in the end, death will overcome us. Fighting the good fight does not mean we are not going to die. God has programmed it that way. God has planned it that way that life has a beginning and it has an ending. We need to go home to heaven because that is our home. Our stay here on earth is only a training ground four our citizenship in heaven. And the best part of the journey is when we are going home.

That's why when a loved one dies, it should be a time for celebration because our loved one has finally completed the race for life.

I HAVE FINISHED THE RACE

In the first century AD, the Romans and Greeks celebrated the Olympics. The Olympics is where the greatest and the best athletes compete. The athletes spend many months in arduous training preparing for the contest in order to win a prize.

But Paul calls this prize - a crown that will not last. Today, winning Olympic athletes receive medals either gold, silver or bronze.

According to St. Paul, finishing the race is like accomplishing a task of testifying to the Gospel of God's grace found in Jesus Christ our Lord. That he had accomplished his mission by sharing Christ to a dying world who needs his love and forgiveness.

In 1984, I watched on TV the summer Olympics held in Los Angeles, California. The women's marathon (26.5 miles) was a great spectacle. There were 44 women contestants.

The gold medalist of that women's marathon was Joan Benoit of Boston, Mass. All the contestants have already reached the finish line except one athlete from Switzerland named Gabriela Andersen Skeiss. She was struggling and agonizing to reach the finish line. She was limping, huffing and puffing as she agonized to reach the finish line. The eyes of the world were focused on her as she strived to reach the finish line.

And as soon as she reached the finish line, she collapsed.

What an athlete! That is the essence of finishing the race.

The Christian life is a commitment to run and finish the race to the finish.

FINALLY, THE APOSTLE PAUL SAYS, "I HAVE KEPT THE FAITH."

Faith is what? Was he talking about faith in the stock market? NO. Was he talking about faith in the economy? NO. Was he talking about faith in our own strength and wisdom? NO.

The Apostle Paul is talking about FAITH IN JESUS CHRIST. I HAVE KEPT THE FAITH. In Galatians 2:20 Paul says, "I have been crucified with Christ. It is no longer I who lives in me and the life I now live in the flesh, I live it by faith in Christ Jesus who loved me and gave himself to me." Without faith in Jesus Christ, we will never reach the finish line. You might be thinking that when we die, you have finally reached the finish line. NO.

When we die, we are just finished, the end of our existence in this life. But without faith in Christ we will never reach the finish line. But where is the finish line anyway? How do we finish the race if we don't see the finish line? Just where is the finish line anyway?

In 1952, young Florence Chadwick tried to swim the waters of the Pacific Ocean starting from the shore of Catalina Island to the shore of California in the West Coast. Florence Chadwick had been the first woman to swim the English Channel both ways. The weather was foggy and chilly, and she could hardly see the boats accompanying her. She had been swimming for more than 15 hours when she begged to be taken out of the water. Her mother, in a boat alongside, told her she was close to the finish line and she could make it. Physically and emotionally exhausted, Florence Chadwick stopped swimming and they pulled her out of the water.

While on the boat she discovered that the shore of California was less than half a mile away. At the news conference the following day, she said, "ALL I COULD SEE WAS THE FOG. I THINK IF I COULD HAVE SEEN THE SHORE, I WOULD HAVE MADE IT."

And that is our problem. WE DON'T SEE THE FINISH LINE. We are like those athletes sitting on a long sleek boats whose movements are synchronized as they pulled those long oars through the water. Those athletes have their backs to the finish line and they could not see the finish line. So how do they know when to row their oars or stop rowing? The answer is they focus on one person sitting at the end of the boat facing the crew. He is called the COXSWAIN. He is the only one who knows where the finish line is. So the men on the oars look to him, obey his commands and count on him to coach them to the finish line. He encourages them, guides them, and directs them. The rowers of the oars are counting on the COXSWAIN to enable them to reach the finish line.

The same is true in the race of life. We don't see the finish line. But we can only focus our eyes on the Lord Jesus Christ who know where the finish line is. In the Book of Hebrews 12:2, we read, "Let us focus our eyes on the Lord Jesus Christ who is the author and finisher of our faith." WHERE IS THE FINISH LINE? THE FINISH LINE IS NO OTHER THAN JESUS CHRIST HIMSELF. Jesus said, "I AM THE WAY, THE TRUTH, AND THE LIFE; NO ONE COMES TO THE FATHER EXCEPT THROUGH ME." (John 14:6) Paul says, "I have kept the faith."

Do you have this faith in Jesus Christ? Do you know him as Lord and savior? If you have not received him yet as Lord and savior of your life, the goodness is that it is never too late.

Don't go home without this assurance of your salvation.

Pray to the Lord like this: "Lord I am sorry for all my sins. Please forgive me and cleanse me from all my sins through the power of the Holy Spirit. Give me the strength to commit my life to you the rest of my life. In Jesus' name. Amen."

When we have prayed that prayer then we can say with St. Paul, "I HAVE FOUGHT A GOOD FIGHT, I HAVE FINISHED THE RACE. I HAVE KEPT THE FAITH."

WE PRAISE AND THANK GOD THAT OUR LOVED ONE WHO DIED IN CHRIST IS FINALLY HOME AT LAST! THANK GOD OUR LOVED, ONE IS HOME AT LAST WITH THE LORD!

In the name of the Father and the Son and the Holy Spirit, Amen.

A Letter of Authorization

I am authorizing you to reprint chapter 19 of my book, The Most Important Thing in Life. Furthermore, you have my permission to use any of my books to meet your purpose. I congratulate you in advance for your next book.

For you I am praying.
Sincerely,
Pastor Dancel

My Own Self-Talk Daily

I thank and praise the Lord for all the blessings in the past, in the present and in the future.

I have a solid faith that I will live a long healthy life by changing the way I think, live, act, feel, eat and handle stress, and I am capable of doing all that.

I pray hard everyday, for the benefit of not only for me, but also for my family, my friends, even for people who hurt me, to overcome our circumstances and for those who died, for the Lord to take them to heaven to enjoy everlasting happiness.

I appreciate the love of my children and all the relationships in my life with whole-hearted gratitude as the greatest inspiration of what I have become.

I strongly avoid scammers that promise all that easy money without the conventional effort on my part, as one of the best ways to de-stress myself.

I will do my best to save as much as I can afford and to be frugal in my spending and be contented of what I have. However, I don't neglect to seriously scrutinize any unusual opportunity that comes along my way.

I believed that my life is my gift from God, and what I can do with my life is my gift to God, and in my own little way, I can share His Love and His Gospel to the people of the world.

I believed that complete happiness is only achieved after death when the Lord takes us with Him to eternal and everlasting happiness, and we have our whole lifetime to prepare for all that.

By doing all these, I can say at the end of my earth's journey, "I did my best, kept the faith, and achieved my dreams!"

Ariston Pallugna Awitan, Jr., M.D.

Acknowledgement

I would like to recognize and acknowledge all the people that helped make this book, especially EWTN - Eternal Word Television Network, Daughters of Saint Paul, St. Anthony Development and Learning Center, Association of Marian Helpers, Priests of the Sacred Heart and Sacred Heart Monastery, Missionary of the Poor, Rev. Reggie M. Dancel Jr.

Without them the publication of this book would have not been possible.

About The Author

The author received his Associate in Arts Degree (Pre-Med), from the University of San Carlos, Cebu City, Philippines in 1951-1954; M.D. Degree, from the College of Medicine, the University of the Philippines in 1954-1959; did his Residency in General and Orthopedic Surgery, in the Philippine General Hospital in 1959-1964; served as Senior Resident Physician, Lakeville Hospital, Lakeville Massachusetts, U.S.A. in 1967-1969.

He was licensed to practice Medicine in New Hampshire, New York, and Texas; and did his Residency in Orthopedic Surgery, at Martland Hospital, Newark N.J., U.S.A in 1969-1973; was Certified Diplomate, American Board of Orthopedic Surgery 1973; as fellow of the American College of Surgeons in 1972;

fellow, American Academy of Orthopedic Surgeons in 1973. He did his Private Practice in Pasadena Texas as Orthopedic Surgeon in 1973 -2005; Served as Major, U.S. Army in 1983 -1985; Served as Orthopedic Surgeon, Randall Medical Center, Fort Hood, Texas in 2005-2006; Served as Orthopedic Physician, at Nova Occupational Medicine Center, Houston TX. in 2006 -2012; Became a

Health Researcher of Nutrition, Chronic diseases and Alternative Treatments of Cancer in 2014-2019.

He became an author of 4 books, "Autobiography of Ariston P. Awitan, Jr.; I am a Doctor, My 3 Wives Died from Cancer, I Learned the Truths about Conventional and Alternative Treatments; LEARNING TO STAY HEALTHY and EVANGELIZE WITH ME."

At long last, in my own little way, I venture to say, *"I have fought a good fight. I have finished the race. I have kept the faith."*

Ariston Pallugna Awitan, Jr., M.D.

References

Bible Verses:

New International Version
The Holy Bible
Revised Standard Version
Catholic Edition

Online Citations:

ewtn.com

connect.pauline.org

choir.pauline.org

media.pauline.org

canadahelps.org/en/charities/missionaries-of-the-poor-canada-inc/

https://daughtersofstpaul.com › Who-We-Are

https://www.facebook.com › DaughterStPaul

https://pauline.org › mission

https://www.masslive.com › boston › 2022 › 02 › nuns-from-the-daughters-of-st-paul-convent-become-unlikely-tik-tok-sensations.html

https://www.charitynavigator.org/about-us/

https://marian.org/amh

https://poshusa.org › what-we-do › the-sacred-heart-monastery

https://poshusa.org/what-we-do

https://poshusa.org/what-we-do/devotion-in-action

https://poshusa.org › who-we-are

https://passionist.org ›

https://www.charitynavigator.org › ein › 391243521

The Most Important Thing in Life by: Rev. Reggie M. Dancel Jr.

Living the Christian Life in a Chaotic World by: Rev. Reggie M. Dancel Jr.

Autobiography of Rev. Reggie M. Dancel, Jr.

LEARNING TO STAY HEALTHY by: Ariston Pallugna Awitan, Jr. M.D.

Fr. Ho Lung's People of Hope by: Wendy-Ann Clarke, The Catholic Register, November 27, 2020

www.ingramcontent.com/pod-product-compliance
Lightning Source LLC
LaVergne TN
LVHW010558070526
838199LV00063BA/5008